"Micha
at the :
comfort, balm, and rest to bruised and worn-out
souls. I heartily recommend that you come and
drink deeply of Christ."

Keith Getty, singer and hymnwriter

"This is a small book about a huge Christ—huge in
majesty, yes, but just as huge in mercy, delighting
to love and care for believers, his own precious
body. Every time I read Mike Reeves, I am brought
back to the real Christ, the biblical Christ, the
irresistible Christ. Well worth reading slowly and
distributing abundantly!"

Dane Ortlund, Senior Pastor of
Naperville Presbyterian Church,
Naperville, Illinois, and author,
Gentle and Lowly and *Surprised by Jesus*

Union

Come,
You Weary

Enjoy Christ's
Comfort

Michael Reeves

Come, You Weary: Enjoy Christ's Comfort
© 2025 by Michael Reeves
www.UnionPublishing.org
Bridgend, Wales, United Kingdom

Cover design by somethingmorecreative.com

978-1-7384324-6-2 (paperback)
978-1-7384324-7-9 (eBook)

For Rudy and Lavonne

Contents

Ephesians 1

¹ Paul, an apostle of Christ Jesus by the will of God, To the saints who are in Ephesus, and are faithful in Christ Jesus: ² Grace to you and peace from God our Father and the Lord Jesus Christ.

³ Blessed be the God and Father of our Lord Jesus Christ, who has blessed us in Christ with every spiritual blessing in the heavenly places, ⁴ even as he chose us in him before the foundation of the world, that we should be holy and blameless before him. In love ⁵ he predestined us for adoption to himself as sons through Jesus Christ, according to the purpose of his will, ⁶ to the praise of his glorious grace, with which he has blessed us in the Beloved. ⁷ In him we have redemption through his blood, the forgiveness of our trespasses, according to the riches of his grace, ⁸ which he lavished upon us, in all wisdom and insight ⁹ making known to us

the mystery of his will, according to his purpose, which he set forth in Christ [10] as a plan for the fullness of time, to unite all things in him, things in heaven and things on earth.

[11] In him we have obtained an inheritance, having been predestined according to the purpose of him who works all things according to the counsel of his will, [12] so that we who were the first to hope in Christ might be to the praise of his glory. [13] In him you also, when you heard the word of truth, the gospel of your salvation, and believed in him, were sealed with the promised Holy Spirit, [14] who is the guarantee of our inheritance until we acquire possession of it, to the praise of his glory.

[15] For this reason, because I have heard of your faith in the Lord Jesus and your love toward all the saints, [16] I do not cease to give thanks for you, remembering you in my prayers, [17] that the God of our Lord Jesus Christ, the Father of glory, may give you the Spirit of wisdom and of revelation in the knowledge of him, [18] having the eyes of your hearts enlightened, that you may know what is the hope to which he has called you, what are the riches of

his glorious inheritance in the saints, [19] and what is the immeasurable greatness of his power toward us who believe, according to the working of his great might [20] that he worked in Christ when he raised him from the dead and seated him at his right hand in the heavenly places, [21] far above all rule and authority and power and dominion, and above every name that is named, not only in this age but also in the one to come. [22] **And he put all things under his feet and gave him as head over all things to the church, [23] which is his body, the fullness of him who fills all in all.**

1

Come and Drink Deeply

"Come, everyone who thirsts,
come to the waters;
and he who has no money,
come, buy and eat!
Come, buy wine and milk
without money and without price."
Isaiah 55:1

Do you feel depleted and fed up right now? Weary in doing good? As if being a Christian is an effort, just too hard to be worth it?

Does the idea of building Christ's church and the thought of mission feel like a burden to you? Do you warm to the reassuring promise from Scripture: "I will build my church" (Matt. 16:18), but in reality, in yourself, you're tired, maybe even spent?

Of course, you want Christ to build his church. But all you're feeling is weakness and coldness. The building of the church is a worthy goal, but frankly, given where you are right now, you feel it's a task you could do without, a job for someone else.

What can make the weary Christian come alive again? What can lift us out of our sense of drudgery, curing our cold and flattened hearts?

The reality is that we will only be as full as the well we drink from.

What follows is an invitation to everyone who thirsts. To you, today—wherever you are and whatever you are feeling. Come to the waters. Come, without money and without price. Don't let your emptiness become a constant state, but recognise it as a thirst, and drink deeply from this fountain.

Drink deeply as you contemplate the sight, the vision, that transforms from glory to glory.

2
Fresh Vision

"Turn to me and be saved,
all the ends of the earth!"
Isaiah 45:22

Let's cut to the chase. If you are fed up, weary, or depleted, or even all three, then one thing can transform you, and one thing only: the source of life itself.

At this spring can be found life for all, not just for the strong and the fit. What you badly need is a fresh sight of the glory of Christ. A fresh vision of the light that overcomes all darkness. The fountain of life itself.

"Turn to me and be saved, all the ends of the earth," Christ says. "Look to me." "Face me." For, beholding him, the glory of the Lord, we are transformed. We are glorified, healed, awakened, brightened, vivified.

"Turn to me." That's it! If you are feeling spiritually low right now, then know for sure that you cannot heal yourself. Not one of us can breathe life into ourselves, however hard we try. Our spiritual sloth is a lack, a void that we cannot fill. Hard work, coffee, talent, excellent church programmes only go so far. They are quick fixes and temporary. They merely mask the problem that we face when we're empty. What we need instead is to experience the life that is found only in Christ.

We need a fresh vision: the enlightening sight of the glory that confers vitality. And that is exactly what Paul gives us in these words describing God's exaltation of Christ:

> He put all things under his feet and gave him as head over all things to the church, which is his body, the fullness of him who fills all in all. (Eph. 1:22–23)

This glorious reality—the wellspring of the chapters that follow—offers a sweet resting place for our bruised and weary souls. But before we press in to enjoy this comfort, please pause to read the fuller context of these words, found in the first chapter of Ephesians (see pages 9–11).

In verses 22–23, Paul lays before us what the Epistle to the Hebrews calls "a sure and steadfast anchor of the soul" (6:19). Here we have a glimpse, by faith, of Jesus in his glory "behind the curtain." This very sight is one that those who are redeemed are enjoying in heaven right now. They see it, and they erupt in worship, crying, "Worthy is the Lamb who was slain, to receive power and wealth and wisdom and might and honor and glory and blessing!" (Rev. 5:12)

Let's turn our gaze in the same direction.

"And he put all things under his feet"—aren't those initial words quite striking? But aren't they also strange? They are strange because we cannot help but wonder, "Weren't all things *always* under his feet?"

Yes indeed, for the Son is Lord by nature. He is the Word, the arm of the Lord, and "by him all things were created, in heaven and on earth, visible and invisible, whether thrones or dominions or rulers or authorities—all things were created through him and for him. And he is before all things, and in him all things hold together" (Col. 1:16–17).

He is the logic and lord of all reality. And not only is he the Word through whom the cosmos was brought into being, but he is the Word through whom *the church* was brought into being. He is the source of life itself, preceding all.

So then, in this context, how does the Father "put all things under [Christ's] feet"? Philippians 2:6–9 throws more light on this:

Though he was in the form of God, [Christ Jesus] did not count equality with God a thing to be grasped, but emptied himself, by taking the form of a servant, being born in the likeness of men. And being found in human form, he humbled himself by becoming obedient to the point of death, even death on a cross. *Therefore* God has highly exalted him and bestowed on him the name that is above every name. (emphasis added)

Here we see something that is absolutely crucial to our sight of Christ. The One who is Lord by nature becomes flesh so that in human flesh he can then be made Lord by being exalted. He takes the humanity that was ruined by the fall (Genesis 3), and he recovers Adam's dominion. He defeats the power of sin and triumphs over our every enemy, leading captivity captive (Eph. 4:8).

Yes, every rule and authority, every power and dominion, every name that is named—sin, death, hell—all have been subjugated to this last Adam, the man Jesus Christ (1 Cor. 15:45; Eph. 1:21). So, that is the sense in which, as Peter put it at Pentecost, "God has *made him* both Lord and Christ, this Jesus whom you crucified" (Acts 2:36; emphasis added).

Of course, in Ephesus, the great name to be named was that of the goddess Artemis. "Great is Artemis of the Ephesians," roared the mob in Acts 19 (v. 28). But where is Artemis now? Nowhere to be seen! She's merely a minor historical curiosity. And so too it will be with every single idol, every human and spiritual power that raises itself against God.

We may forget this, but we can be sure that the devils don't. This was why they would shriek when they encountered Jesus. Like Dagon, toppled before the ark (1 Sam. 5:1–5), all fall under the feet of this victorious Man. And all heaven watches as this Man rises from humiliation and death, and the angels cry,

> "Lift up your heads, O gates!
>> And lift them up, O ancient doors,
>> that the King of glory may come in."
>>> (Ps. 24:9)

The Father then says to him,

> "Sit at my right hand,
>> until I make your enemies
>> a footstool."
> The LORD sends forth from Zion
>> your mighty scepter.
>> Rule in the midst of your enemies!"
>>> (Ps. 110:1–2)

But why is this so significant, and what difference will it all make in the lives of fatigued and jaded believers today?

3
Unexpected Standing

"Sit at my right hand, until I make
your enemies your footstool."
Psalm 110:1

When the Father says to the eternal Son, "Sit at my right hand," so that all things are under his feet, this is not an exaltation to new heights. The Son is returning home to his Father's side. He is taking the place on the throne that has always been his by right.

But something has changed; something is completely different. As the Son sits in his rightful place, he does so now in human flesh, taking humanity in himself, so that for the first time ever it is a *man* who sits on the throne at the right hand of

God. Now a human can call God "Father." Christ's exaltation as man, then, is for *our* sakes—for otherwise, why would the eternal Son need exalting? He does this for the church, which is his body. In Christ's exaltation as man, we too are exalted.

So, for the first time ever, a man enjoys the Son's own fellowship with, and his standing before, the Father. Amazingly, this is the son of Mary, the adopted son of a carpenter, now sitting on the throne of the universe. And this man now sits no longer as a victim to the serpent's wiles, but as a true king, utterly victorious. In him, Psalm 8:4–8 is surely fulfilled:

> What is man that you are mindful of him, and the son of man that you care for him? Yet you have made him a little lower than the heavenly beings and crowned him with glory and honor. You have given him dominion over the works of your hands; you have put all things under his feet, all sheep and oxen, and also the beasts of the field, the birds of the heavens, and the fish of the sea, whatever passes along the paths of the seas.

Significantly, this kingly triumph of Christ's would mean the fulfilment of what Adam was initially created to be.

So, in this putting of "all things under [Christ's] feet," we see God's grace in how he shares the Son's own life with us. In him, we see what kind of lord is Lord. We see an utterly unexpected glory: the glory of one who delights to spread his goodness. And wonderfully, mercifully, it is his glory to save sinners to the uttermost, to raise the dead, and to exalt a people who deserve nothing but judgment.

Who would ever have expected this? Cowering in our guilt, we could never have dared to imagine such radiant kindness. This is a glory beyond transcendence: God wielding power in grace to his people. Majestically compassionate, this God is dazzling in the overflowing superabundance of his very being and blessedness.

Even as believers, when we think of Christ enthroned, we can so easily think of him as distant and aloof. For that is how power normally is and how it usually behaves. And so, we are quick to assume that the compassion and humility he had on earth were left behind when he was exalted to heaven. Yet the one enthroned is the same Jesus that we know, our Brother, in the body that was pierced for our transgressions. He is the very same one whom we have seen with our eyes, whom we have looked upon and have touched with our hands (1 John 1:1).

Christ, the last Adam, ascends back to where the first Adam was: with God. In Exodus, God commanded his people concerning the crops they harvest, "The best of the firstfruits of your ground you shall bring into the house of the LORD your God." (23:19). Now it is Christ himself who is the "firstfruits" and forerunner of the new humanity, taken into the house of the Lord. And he is seated there with our flesh and blood, our experiences of the world, our humanity, in heaven.

What an encouragement to us today as we gaze upon him! He has ascended; he is seated on high; God has "put all things under his feet." But he is neither distant nor aloof. He has lifted us up in himself.

Let us now turn to the implications of this for you and me today. How can we be in him, and he in us?

4

Sympathetic Friend and Brother

"There is a friend who sticks
closer than a brother."
Proverbs 18:24

On the throne of grace, we have a lord and a great
high priest who can sympathise with our weak-
nesses, having been tempted in every way like us
(Heb. 4:14–16). And having experienced on earth
every form of pain, rejection, and sorrow, Christ
in heaven is moved by our struggles more deeply
than the most loving family member or friend we
can think of. He's a lionlike Lord, to be sure, but
he's also a Lamb, looking "as though it had been
slain" (Rev. 5:6). And he's a Lord who has made
himself our brother, or, as we see above, "a friend

who sticks *closer than* a brother" (emphasis added).

The Heidelberg Catechism asks,

What *comfort* is it to you that Christ "shall come again to judge the living and the dead"?

Answer: That in all my sorrows and persecutions, with uplifted head I look for *the very same person*, who has before offered himself for me to the judgment of God, and has removed all curse from me, to come again as judge from heaven.[1] (emphasis added)

Weary, stumbling Christian, since Christ has shed his blood for you, do you really think he could not care about you? That you are alone in your weariness and distress? He humbled himself for us; he endured the most awful suffering, rejection, and death for us; and he was exalted for us, to bring us to glory.

---

1   Heidelberg Catechism, Lord's Day 19. The phrase set off by quotation marks is from the Nicene Creed and references 2 Timothy 4:1.

Stop and consider that for a moment: what it meant for him, and what it means for us too. Dane Ortlund puts it beautifully in *Deeper*:

> He who is both Lion and Lamb is both transcendent and immanent, both far and near, both great and good—both King and Friend.
>
> What does a friend do? A friend draws near in time of need. A friend delights to come into solidarity with us, bearing our burdens. A friend listens. A friend is available to us, never too high or important to give us time. A friend shares his deepest heart.[2]

No wonder that at a time of deep sorrow, Joseph Scriven could pen the hymn: "What a Friend We Have in Jesus."

No wonder that in heaven, where the redeemed can see Christ most clearly and appreciate him even more, no one can help but cry, "Worthy is the Lamb who was slain" (Rev. 5:12).

---

2 Dane C. Ortlund, *Deeper: Real Change for Real Sinners* (Wheaton, IL: Crossway, 2022), 27–28.

5

Exalted Head
Over All Things

"My beloved is mine, and I am his."
Song of Solomon 2:16

A lord. A high priest. A lamb. A brother. A friend.

That's huge—but that's not all! This beautiful exalted one: God then *gave him* as a gift to the church (Eph. 1:22). Just as God gave his only Son to be with us in our humiliation, God gave him to the church so that we might be with him in his triumph.

Christ is a good head, a good husband, so he will enjoy nothing without his spouse, the church. When she was poor, he became poor for her sake. When she was despised, he too was spat upon.

And now that he is in heaven, he must have her there along with him. If he sits on a throne, then she too must have a throne. If he has fullness of joy and honour and glory forever, then so must she. He will not be in heaven and simply leave her behind. And he will not enjoy a single privilege of heaven without her being a sharer with him.

Isn't that good to know? Christ doesn't separate his greatness from his spouse. Far from it! He makes his own dignity hers. All that is his is ours. And so, since all things are under *his* feet, by giving Christ "as head over all things to the church, which is his body," the Lord has put all things under *his people's* feet.

What does this mean? It means that our sins and corruptions, our sorrows and afflictions, this world and the world to come are all made subject unto us. And all the immeasurable greatness of that divine power that raised Jesus from the dead is now wielded towards you, to keep you safe for the hope to which he has called you.

And ultimately—soon, according to Romans 16:20—"the God of peace will … crush Satan under your feet." For, united to our exalted head, we will reign in life forever.

6

Mountain-Top Gospel Perspective

"Having the eyes of your hearts enlightened, that you may know
what is the hope to which he has called you, what are the riches of
his glorious inheritance in the saints, and what is the immeasurable
greatness of his power toward us who believe."
Ephesians 1:18–19

As Paul sees it, many of the troubles we have in the
Christian life come from a lack of knowledge. Or
maybe we should say *ignored* knowledge, a knowledge besmeared with a worldly outlook. We don't
have a sufficiently God-centred, gospel-shaped
perspective, and without that, our faith becomes
weak and stunted.

Because of this, we struggle to "rejoice always"
(1 Thess. 5:16). Like the rest of the world, we fret.
We forget how supremely blessed and cared for we
are. That's why Paul's chief concern for Christians

is that they might grow in the knowledge of God, and in a maintained clarity of that God-centred perspective.

Have you ever climbed a mountain and viewed a nearby town or city from the summit? Were you surprised by how different it seemed from this new angle?

Let's revisit the mountain-top of Ephesians 1:22–23: "And he put all things under his feet and gave him as head over all things to the church, which is his body, the fullness of him who fills all in all."

Paul's purpose in the final verses of Ephesians 1 (vv. 15–23) is to encourage struggling Christians and to pray that they might also know his glorious mountain-top gospel perspective.

There is something here that is particularly comforting for us as believers. Note the importance of the church, and see just how highly Christ and his Father value it. All things are put under Christ's feet, and he is given "as head over all things to the church," for she is his great concern. The church means more to him than all his dominion over the world.

We've known this high priority already from

Christ's High Priestly Prayer in John 17, where Christ prays to his Father not for the world, but for those whom the Father has given him. He prays, "Father, ... glorify your Son that the Son may glorify you, since you have given him authority over all flesh, to give eternal life to all whom you have given him" (vv. 1–2). His authority over all flesh is exerted for the church.

What a perspective of faith, when to the eyes of the world around us the church seems so utterly insignificant and perilously fragile! If God is for us, who can be against us? No wonder we need to refresh ourselves in this life-giving truth. Christ rules all things *for the church*. Creation and providence are for the church. From his throne of love, he steers every atom and every superpower ultimately for the good of his people. When God's enemies seek to frustrate his purposes (like Judas and Pilate did), they only succeed in fulfilling them. For every creature, whatever its aim, is executing God's purposes. If we could see the final end, all are doing what we would wish them to do.

That's why the Puritan John Flavel was able to write:

Could saints but see what fruits their
    troubles bring,
Amidst those troubles they would
    shout and sing.
O sacred wisdom! who can but admire
To see how thou dost save from fire, by fire!
No doubt but saints in glory wond'ring stand
At those strange methods few now
    understand.[1]

Therefore, brothers and sisters, our labour in the Lord is not in vain. It is part of the victory of Jesus Christ that will one day be manifest for what it is. Such a realisation, such anticipation can cause great saints to "shout and sing" at "sacred wisdom" in spite of their sore troubles.

In the light of all that we have seen, it can be no surprise to learn that our labour does not need to be a burden we carry all by ourselves. And isn't that the weight which so often grinds us down, leading to so much stress and burnout in the church?

We labour as if the victory were not ours already, and we work as if everything were up to us.

---

1 John Flavel, *Navigation Spiritualized*, in *The Works of John Flavel*, vol. 5 (repr., Edinburgh: The Banner of Truth Trust, 1968), 280.

As if we were necessary. As if everything would fall apart if we didn't perform "just so."

God the Father has happily left the government of the world in the hands of Christ. You too can leave all your concerns in his hands. Remember how he *cares*. Those who touch the saints touch the apple of his eye. He wields all for his beloved.

7

Inseparable Union

"We are members of his body."
Ephesians 5:30

And who *is* Christ's beloved? Paul's next words in Ephesians 1:22–23 tell us: she is "the church, which is his body, the fullness of him who fills all in all." What Paul shows us here is that Jesus Christ has a double headship. He is, first of all, head over all things—head of the world—*by dominion*; and second, he is head of the church *by union*. But he is head of the church in a connected, attached, organic, and quite different way from the way in which he is head of the world.

Christ's headship over the world is one of

authority and reign. But when Paul says that Christ is head over the church, he means that Christ is the head of a body. And like a body with a head, the church is inseparably united to him. So, Christ cannot now be pulled apart from his church. He has not just been given to the church—he has become "one flesh" with his people.

This is why Paul himself once heard those memorable words on the Damascus Road: "Saul, Saul, why are you persecuting *me*?" (Acts 9:4; emphasis added). For what is hers—her trials, her sorrows—must also be his. And what is his must be hers. As the head breathes, the body lives. So too the church derives her life and breath from him.

As the oil ran down from Aaron's head to his body when he was anointed as high priest (Lev. 8:12; Ps. 133:2), so we are partakers of Christ's anointing. Without measure or limit, we receive the Spirit with which he is filled. And filled with his Spirit, the body, the church, shares in Christ's priestly intercessory ministry. She shares his authority to forgive sins—the keys of the kingdom. She shares his prophetic ministry, heralding his self-revelation to the world.

And she shares in his triumph *over* the world. She will one day share his kingly reign. Christ arms and equips his body with his own life-giving power. He adorns his body with his own heavenly beauty. He enriches her with his wealth. He shares with her *all* that he has received from the Father.

8

Heavenly Bridegroom

"I saw the holy city, new Jerusalem, coming down out of heaven from God, prepared as a bride adorned for her husband."
Revelation 21:2

You will have noticed that I keep referring to the body as "her," and earlier I spoke of "husband," "beloved," and "spouse" as well. Why is that? Because, of course, the language of "head" and "body" is not just corporeal but marital language.

And this is where the first chapter of Ephesians has been heading all along: the triune God's plan, from before the foundation of the world, has all been geared towards his bride, moving towards the marriage of the Lamb. Christ's headship over all things has been for his headship of his body, his spouse: "The church, which is his body... ." This is what Paul goes on to call the "profound" mystery of Christ and his church (Eph. 5:32).

So, when the first man Adam cleaves to his wife and becomes one with her, Adam is, as God says, a pattern of the one to come (Gen. 2:24). The first marriage is a picture of the last marriage, the ultimate one, when the church will appear as a bride beautifully prepared for her husband (Rev. 21:2).

Eve was taken from Adam's side, and the Lord literally *built* the woman (the actual Hebrew term of construction used in Genesis 2:22). So too, the Lord says, "I will build my church" (Matt. 16:18), and she will be built out of him, deriving her very being and nature from him.

She is the joy for which he endured the cross. His desire was not just for a return to a heavenly glory that he had always had, for to do that, he would not have had to undergo the cross.

Rather, the Lord's purpose had always been that an object of righteousness and praise might sprout up before all the nations (Isa. 61:11). He had always intended that her righteousness might go forth as brightness, and her salvation as a burning torch (Isa. 62:1). And that the nations might see her righteousness, and all the kings should see her glory (Isa. 62:2). This is the heavenly bridegroom: one who will not rest, will not stop, until his bride is glorified and all the world gasps at her beauty.

It is so striking that Isaiah can use the language of *her* righteousness and *her* glory. The nations shall see *her* righteousness, *her* brightness. For this is the nature of *his* radiant glory. In *his* righteousness, he makes *her* righteous. In *his* beauty, he makes *her* beautiful. How? Because all that he is he gives to her, and all that he has he shares with her. She is his body.

He takes our sin; we take his righteousness. And so, his bride can share those beautiful words in Isaiah 61:10: "I will greatly rejoice in the LORD; my soul shall exult in my God, for he has clothed me with the garments of salvation; he has covered me with the robe of righteousness … as a bride adorns herself with her jewels."

Christ is such an overwhelmingly loving husband that he tells his bride, "You shall be a crown of beauty in the hand of the LORD, and a royal diadem in the hand of your God" (Isa. 62:3). A crown is the most precious of treasures. It is a reward for great victors and conquerors. It is the highest sign of honour for its wearer. And Proverbs 12:4 says, "An excellent wife is the crown of her husband."

The church is the excellent wife, the crown, of Jesus Christ. She is his most precious treasure, the reward for his great victory. The church is the sign of just who he is—the One who awakens the dead, saves the helpless, and draws humankind together in love. The church is the great testimony of who Jesus is. She is his crown, his glory.

In the church, a divine glory is displayed for all the world to see. She is a taste of heaven come to earth. And Christ says to her, "You shall be called My *Delight* Is in Her, and your land Married; for the LORD *delights* in you, and your land shall be married. For as a young man marries a young woman, so shall your sons marry you, and as the bridegroom rejoices over the bride, so shall your God rejoice over you" (Isa. 62:4–5; emphasis added).

This head does not simply have pity on his bride. No, he has the most passionate love for and delight in her. She *thrills* him. The thought of her enjoying and reflecting his glory was why he brought the whole cosmos into being.

9

Divine Goodness, Spread and Shared

"The fountain of living waters."
Jeremiah 2:13

As Paul goes on to say, Christ's beloved, his body, is "the fullness of him who fills all in all" (Eph. 1:23). "The fullness of him"? Yes, for the church is the expression of God's overflowing fullness. Obviously, that's not to say that Christ lacks anything in himself. After all, he is not "served by human hands, as though he needed anything" (Acts 17:25). Neither is he lonely or bored. No, for "in him all the fullness of God was pleased to dwell" (Col. 1:19). Here's how the great Puritan Richard Sibbes expressed it:

If God had not a communicative, spreading goodness, he would never have created the world. The Father, Son, and Holy Ghost were happy in themselves, and enjoyed one another before the world was. Apart from the fact that God delights to communicate and spread his goodness, there would never have been a creation or redemption.[1]

Here, Sibbes was saying that God didn't need to create the world either to satisfy himself or to *be* himself. Christ did not need to redeem us in order to be full. The Father, Son, and Spirit "were happy in themselves, and enjoyed one another before the world was." Rather, God is like a warming sun of life who "delights to spread his beams ... . Such a goodness is in God as is in a fountain, or in the breast that loves to ease itself of milk."[2] In other words, God didn't create and Christ didn't redeem because he needed to, nor because of any lack.

Instead, God in Christ went out to create and redeem *because* he was so happily self-existent, so

1   Richard Sibbes, *The Bruised Reed*, ed. Banner of Truth Trust (Edinburgh: Banner of Truth, 1998), 3.
2   Sibbes, *The Bruised Reed*, 2.

bursting with goodness. God was so overflowingly, superabundantly full of life in himself that he delighted to spread his goodness. And the church is the faithful witness, the testimony to that fullness to be found in her "head," so that "through the church the manifold wisdom of God might now be made known to the rulers and authorities in the heavenly places" (Eph. 3:10).

She is the evidence that the head over all things is not a parsimonious lord. Far from it! Rather, he has life in himself—and so much so that he is brimming over with it. He is "the fountain of living waters" (Jer. 2:13), the one whose very life, being, and goodness is radiant and outgoing, spreading out that there might be more that is truly good. He is "the radiance of the glory of God" (Heb. 1:3), going out from the Father, in grace, to *communicate* glory.

This is our God: a beautiful, overflowing fountain of life and goodness. And we are the thirsty ones, invited to drink freely, deeply, and long.

10

Glory That
Fills All Things

"For the earth will be filled
with the knowledge of the glory of the LORD
as the waters cover the sea."
Habakkuk 2:14

As Paul reaches the climax at the end of Ephesians 1, it seems that the higher he goes, the more dense and rich and overwhelming his thinking becomes. No wonder that the meaning of his final phrase—"the fullness of him who fills all in all" (v. 23)—is something that commentators struggle to agree on. For does Paul mean that Christ fills all things in the sense that he is head over all things *in the universe*? Or does "all" here mean "all" in the church—in other words, that he fills *all his body*?

Now, both of these interpretations are true, of

course, but I think that Paul's thought here is richer and weightier than either of those single ingredients. Yes, Christ is head over all things, and he fills his body now just as the glory of the Lord once filled the temple of the Lord. But it is only when we read it all together that the full scope of Paul's meaning becomes clear: the church is "the *fullness of him who fills* all in all." So, the *way in which* he fills cannot be separated from his fullness.

Christ fills all things *with his fullness*, which is his bride. In other words, the body of Christ is the fullness with which Christ fills all things. This is an idea that Paul comes back to in Ephesians 4, from verse 8:

> Therefore it says,
>
> > "When he ascended on high he
> > led a host of captives,
> > and he gave gifts to men."
>
> (In saying, "He ascended," what does it mean but that he had also descended into the lower regions, the earth? He who descended is the one who also ascended far above all the heavens, *that he might fill all things*.)

And he gave the apostles, the prophets, the evangelists, the shepherds and teachers, to equip the saints for the work of ministry, *for building up the body of Christ.* (vv. 8–12; emphasis added)

How, in this context, does Christ come to "fill all things"? He does it by giving the Spirit in his ascension, and so giving spiritual gifts to equip the saints *to build up the body of Christ.*

God had said to the first Adam, "Be fruitful and multiply and fill the earth and subdue it, and have dominion over the fish of the sea and over the birds of the heavens and over every living thing that moves on the earth" (Gen. 1:28). "Fill the earth" meant "Be fruitful and multiply."

And through his church, Christ fulfils that primary mandate. He is fruitful; his church grows; and so his fullness fills the earth. Because the arm of the Lord was revealed in Isaiah 53 as a man of sorrows who bore our griefs and who was pierced for our transgressions. And because this man was high and lifted up and exalted, so the Lord says to his barren people in Isaiah 54,

Enlarge the place of your tent,
      and let the curtains of your habitations
      be stretched out;
do not hold back; lengthen your cords
      and strengthen your stakes.
For you will spread abroad to the right
        and to the left,
      and your offspring will possess
        the nations
      and will people the desolate cities.
"Fear not, … .
For your Maker is your husband,
      the Lord of hosts is his name;
and the Holy One of Israel is your Redeemer,
      the God of the whole earth he is called.
                      (vv. 2–5)

And so, the glory that fills the temple, the body of Christ, flames out to fill all things. Through the church, Christ fills the universe with his glory. She spreads abroad and possesses the nations. Then, as Paul writes in 2 Thessalonians 1:10, Christ will be "glorified in his saints." He will irradiate them with his glory. He will shine forth in them as the fullness of his glory, and in them he will be glorified in all the earth.

> The LORD will arise upon you,
>> and his glory will be seen upon you.
> And nations shall come to your light,
>> and kings to the brightness of
>>> your rising. …
> Then you shall see and be radiant;
>> your heart shall thrill and exult,
> because the abundance of the sea
>> shall be turned to you,
>> the wealth of the nations shall come to
>>> you. (Isa. 60:2–3, 5)

So, the very creation of the world and all God's providences find their end in the day of the gladness of Christ's heart, when he rejoices in his bride and his bride rejoices in him, and he is glorified in the perfection of his work.

Brothers and sisters, what a head we have in Jesus. In him all the fullness of the Godhead dwells: above all, filling all in all, he has been given to the church so that we too might have his fullness. Fullness is found in him. And *only* in him.

11
Come!

"Jesus stood up and cried out, 'If anyone thirsts,
let him come to me and drink.'"
John 7:37

"Come to me." "Turn to me." This is the call of our glorious, good, and loving Saviour to anyone who thirsts, anyone who lacks. To all who are weary.

Fullness is not found anywhere in creation. It can only ever be found in Christ.

Of course, as bodily creatures, we still need rest and relaxation and pleasure so that we do not burn out or wear out. So, take time to recuperate. Take it regularly. Make time for friends. Rest, recuperation, and friendship have their place. They are all good gifts from our good Father. We ignore them at our peril.

But there is no life without Christ. However much we try to rest, without him we will shrivel and wear out.

Remember, you will only be as full as the well you drink from. So come, everyone who thirsts, come to the waters; come, without money and without price. Don't let your emptiness become a constant state, but recognise it as a thirst, and drink deeply from this fountain. Contemplate, and contemplate again, the sight that transforms from glory to glory.

And know that as you do so, Christ will reign until all his enemies are his footstool. While he awaits that day, he will hold his bride in his tender arms until she is prepared and "her righteousness goes forth as brightness, and her salvation as a burning torch" (Isa. 62:1).

And so let us make Paul's prayer in Ephesians 3:17–20 our own:

Father of glory, we praise you for giving us such a head in Christ. Strengthen us with power through your Spirit so that Christ may dwell in our hearts through faith, so that we, being rooted and grounded in love, may have strength to comprehend with all the saints what is the breadth and length and height and depth, and to know the love of Christ that surpasses knowledge, that we may be filled with all the fullness of God.

Now to him who is able to do far more abundantly than all that we ask or think, according to the power at work within us, to him be glory in the church and in Christ Jesus throughout all generations, forever and ever. Amen.

Reflect or Discuss

Chapter 1: Come and Drink Deeply

1. Does it help you to be real about your state of mind, acknowledging any weariness, weakness, or coldness you are feeling and bringing it out into the open?

2. Do you warm to the prospect of a solution that doesn't require self-effort? One that comes from beyond yourself?

Chapter 2: Fresh Vision

1. What is the one thing that can transform the weary, depleted, and fed up?

2. Can you think of a time when you were "awakened," "brightened," or "vivified" by a fresh sight of Christ? How did that inspire or motivate you in your Christian life?

3. As you read this chapter, did you start to glimpse "the enlightening sight of the glory that confers vitality"?

Chapter 3: Unexpected Standing

1. Why is it significant that it is a man who sits on the throne at the right hand of God?
2. What does Christ's recovering of Adam's dominion mean, and how does it change things for us irrevocably?
3. Why would the eternal Son need exalting?

Chapter 4: Sympathetic Friend and Brother

1. How do we know that "Christ in heaven is moved by our struggles" even more deeply than a close friend?
2. Think about the "comfort" in the Heidelberg Catechism that Christ "shall come again to judge the living and the dead." How can this truth from 2 Timothy 4:1 become your resting place?
3. How is Jesus "both Lion and Lamb"? Why is this significant for those who place their trust in him?

Chapter 5: Exalted Head Over All Things

1. We see in Ephesians 1:22 that Christ "will enjoy nothing without his spouse, the church." How does this bring comfort to weary saints today?

2. What will it mean for us as believers in the future (see Rom. 16:20)?

Chapter 6: Mountain-Top Gospel Perspective

1. Using Ephesians 1 and John 17, align your thinking with how Christ views the church.
2. How does this compare with the way that the world around you portrays the church, or even how the church often sees itself?
3. Why should we never be downcast and discouraged by our toil and trouble in this life? And what does it look like to leave our concerns "in the hands of Christ" rather than attempting to bear them alone?

Chapter 7: Inseparable Union

1. What are the implications of our inseparable union with Christ—for our lives and for our worship?
2. What does it mean that Jesus Christ has a double headship?
3. Who is Christ's beloved? How does this affect how we treat her?

Chapter 8: Heavenly Bridegroom

1. What can we learn about Christ from the parallels with the first man, Adam?

2. What difference does it make to know that the church brings joy to Christ?

Chapter 9: Divine Goodness, Spread and Shared

1. Why did God in Christ go out to create and redeem?

2. How does the invitation to drink at "a beautiful, overflowing fountain of life and goodness" enlarge your approach to God in prayer?

Chapter 10: Glory That Fills All Things

1. How does Christ come to "fill all things"?

2. "Christ will be 'glorified in his saints.' He will irradiate them with his glory. He will shine forth in them as the fullness of his glory, and in them he will be glorified in all the earth." Reflect on these words from 2 Thessalonians 1:10. How do they give you a greater perspective on your life / situation / concerns today?

 **Union**Grow

Learn theology and delight in Christ with **trusted teachers.**

Subscribe to Union Grow for unlimited access to Union Publishing's video teaching, eBooks and audiobooks.

TRUTH FOR LIFE

Truth For Life is the Bible teaching ministry of Alistair Begg and a trusted source of biblical truth.

DAILY PROGRAM

Listen to Alistair Begg teach verse by verse through books of the Bible on the daily program *Truth For Life*. Search for *Truth For Life* where you listen to podcasts or on YouTube, download our free mobile app from your app store, listen online at **truthforlife.org**, or find the program on your local radio station by visiting **truthforlife.org/stationfinder**.

DAILY DEVOTIONAL

Begin each day learning from the Bible by listening to a five-minute daily devotional by Alistair Begg. Search for *Truth For Life Daily Devotions* on YouTube or where you listen to podcasts. You can also listen by downloading our mobile app or at **truthforlife. org/devotionals**. If you prefer to read the daily devotional, subscribe to receive it as a free daily email at **truthforlife.org/lists**.

CONTACT TRUTH FOR LIFE

P.O. Box 398000 Cleveland, Ohio 44139
ph. 1 (888) 588-7884   **email** letters@truthforlife.org
web truthforlife.org